The Dragon Slide

by **Gill Britten**

illustrated by **Michael Reid**

Mr Green took the school swimming.

Ranjit, Jamie, Nicky and Beth went.

Ben Jones went, too.

Ben and his friend made a mess on the bus.
"Stop that, Ben!" said Beth.
"Make me!" laughed Ben.

"I don't like Ben Jones," said Beth.

"He's a show off!"

"I heard that, Beth!" said Ben. He was cross.

"I'm going to get you for that!" he said.

Beth was scared.

The bus got to the swimming pool.
Everyone got off the bus. Ben pushed Beth.
"I'm going to get you," said Ben.

Mr Green saw Ben push Beth.

“Stop that, Ben!” he shouted.

They all got into the swimming pool. Jamie went to the dragon slide. He went up to the top of the slide.

Jamie sat down at the top of the slide. WHOOSH! Down the dragon slide he went. SPLASH! Into the pool he went.

Nicky got to the top of the dragon slide. Then he saw Beth in the water. Ben was pushing her.

Nicky went down the dragon slide
into the water.
"Stop that!" Nicky shouted.
"Make me!" shouted Ben.

Mr Green heard Ben. He saw Ben push Nicky.

"Stop that, Ben!" he shouted.

Mr Green was cross.

"Now Mr Green is cross with me!" said Ben. "I'm going to get you for that, Nicky."

Nicky went up the dragon slide. So did Ben and his friend.

Nicky sat down at the top of the slide.

WHOOSH! Down the slide he went.

SPLASH! Into the water he went.

Then there was a big SPLASH! Ben landed on top of Nicky ...

… so did Ben's friend.

Mr Green saw Ben land on top of Nicky.

He was very cross.

"Ben! Get out, now!" he shouted.

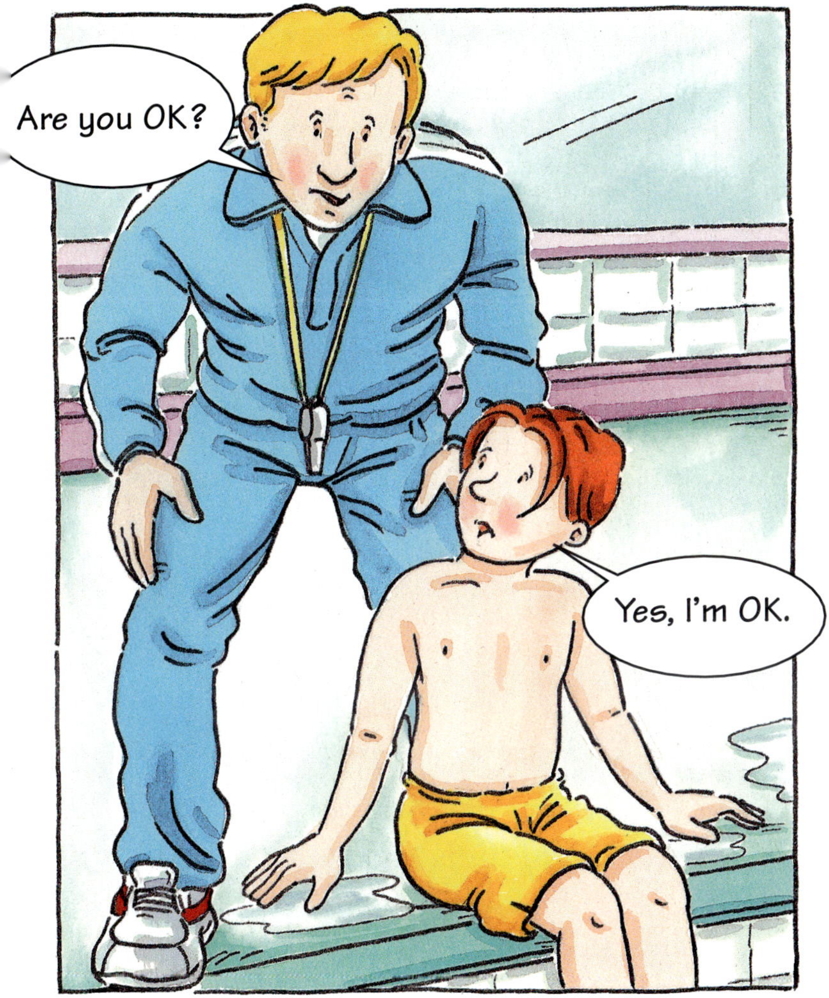

Mr Green helped Nicky.

"Are you OK?" said Mr Green.

"Yes, I'm OK," said Nicky.

Mr Green was cross with Ben and his friend.

"You can't go back into the pool," he said.

"What can I do with you?"

Beth had an idea. She told Mr Green her idea and he laughed.

“Come on, you two!” said Mr Green.

"What did you say to Mr Green?"

said Nicky.

"Wait and see!" said Beth.

They all went back to the dragon slide ...

... and Ben went back to the bus!